After The Storm

AFTER THE STORM

THOMAS ZEMSKY

[signature: Thomas Zemsky]

Broadstone Books

Library of Congress Control Number 2016934725

ISBN 978-1-937968-20-5

The author gratefully acknowledges
The Cincinnati Review
for first publishing "Quickly Aging Here" and "Fall."

Design & Typesetting by Christopher Taylor
Text set in Minion Pro
Cover set in Poor Richard

Broadstone Books
An Imprint of
Broadstone Media LLC
418 Ann Street
Frankfort, Kentucky 40601-1929
BroadstoneBooks.com

Contents

III

I

THE RECIPE

I wonder why there is no recipe these days
for writing poetry like there is
for baking bread.
After all, man's mouth
has forever been filled
with the pleasures of dough & words.
The wheat drinks in a sun
little changed from that
which shone on Homer's sea.
The braided loaves, like the
pale entwined limbs of young Hero & Leander,
swell from a yeast potent as ever.
And finally one is in the presence
of masks, so ancient & fragrant, immortal & sophisticated,
each crusted feature magically different
everytime from one another,
concealing a heart soft & mysterious as any cloud.

The oven door bangs open,
the face is flushed,
& the senses rise
like a pack of wolves to the moon.

And so it is poetry after all.
One writes. And starves.

Poem for Philip Guston

I

Dictators aren't profound.
Children beg for pennies
outside their tombs.
We meet with hands
that keep the rain from rusting pennies.

II

Food pulled from the ground,
love pressed from flesh,
all the ordinary work of hands
that clean by touch, tap & clutch,
stroke, heft, sift, pry, pull, pinch, wipe, rub,
fondle, fret, knead, embrace, winnow & worry, grasp,
grip, caress, thump, turn, squeeze, shape & smooth,
shake, tickle, fashion & design, measure & refine, every surface of life
framed in the dirt-cleansing clay of hands.

III

Other hands. The hands of armies & slaves,
& a thousand thousand
hands at one's command.
Under the roof of sky, only the king's
hands grow dirty with disuse, until the day
they are solemnly wrapped by concubines,
an ordinary day, carried & buried
for the earth to scour & scatter
the bones of the hands....

IV

That faint light
given off by the snow
is the exact age of joy—
unhurried cloud—
glow of rain
in the ground,
in the ground somewhere,
full of emperors' hands each
holding a penny.

OK

Oklahoma irrevocable
& pandaesque,
the sun rolled

out of the earth,
horse bitten skies;
clear water

in a screen door slam,
parade grounds
full of bearded spiders,

wooden seed
casked in burlap,
mouse written floors;

goodnight ice-cream,
owl eyes
without an objective correlative

for a horizon.
The farmer
steps off his porch,
tan in the folds,
and says, "Pants!"

After the Storm

The asylum burned down last night.
For a moment, with the help
of flames and uncomprehending shrieks,
the place grew to fill the contours
our imaginations had for it.
Amazingly, no one was killed:
not one catatonic consumed like a log,
or messianic figure demanding calmly
that the conflagration stop
short of his consecrated flesh.
What had originally been an orphanage,
when life's problems were less abstract,
now lies in ashes and smoldering walls
and parts of stairs as delusional
as its latest occupants, many
of whom wandered off
when the world opened into
the image in their heads
and entered our city—
mad as politicians or childlike
as Mr. Grimalke half asleep
behind his candy counter, intense
as long-distance joggers or happy
as fans of the local college
whose basketball team just won
the conference championship,
O secretive as post office boxes
they will have to be rounded up,
32 of them according to
the director, and when they are,
when they are,
and our town earnestly returns to its love affairs,
and the football season begins,
and even the children start to forget

when people would look suspiciously
at individuals on park benches or
call the manager about the lady
talking to herself
in the lingerie department
at Henderson's, then something commonplace
as a stroke of lightning can claim
the safety of its status as just a miracle again,
though I suspect two or three of us maybe
will understand how life is irrational,
like standing behind bars of rain
and being freed by fire.

CLASSIC POEM

god, it's weird, someone made
a bottle, and someone filled the bottle
up, now that is weird, and someone
tilts that bottle back and thinks he can empty it

The Voyeur

He stands above his own shoulders
to look through the transom
at her stepping from the shower;
and how he aches and trembles
while he imagines a nakedness
with which to clothe the power of her body;
which is where we leave him,
near the ceiling and in the hall,
in an act of disbelief,
that she might teach him
to kneel less precariously,
at a height not measured by a fall.

Ever

I am a horse on a ladder who came down to dance, oh the fool,
my other left foot and then my right, overturning tables,
drinking beer off the floor, while the band plays "it's
lonelier than an orphan, my father needs my mother so,"
& outside my father biting a blind man on the rear,
like the invention of shadows; & I race back up the ladder,
ah the fool, higher than anyone's ever been, so high
I can watch the snow fall on all the lobsters & make big
eyebrows on theater marquees, though I admit it's hard to
ever neigh & race & watch all the snows ever coming home
to a set table, with deep bowls of summer & spoons of ice

Scissors

Reflection that is free
to touch its object;
more dangerous than
reached horizons, coming and going;
hysterical, empty eyed,
whose kiss divides the world;
insidious trap to snare the hand
when it opens, so it may not close again
without memories.

THE WOODSMAN

Moon reckless as the axe
I lean against a tree—
        the day dies down,
                cold and dark as any star

Let sleep find me quiet
        as the felled wood,
    in the vision of this clearing, heart,

Now that your fire delineates
        those forests in my hands,
                        dark as any
                        on which the sun's roots have fed—

What Can I Say?

What can I say about the late world?
The late dinosaur tracks
crossing the late drive-in movie screens.
The late clouds of dust
raised by the late herds of buffalo,
& the late clouds of whooping cranes above them.
The late clouds & the late dust,
& just lately, the late snow to remind us of them both.
The late flowers tall as trees.
The late jackknife laughter at the sight
of bodies ballooned into mad shapes
like something haunted even while sunned.
The late magic on & off of streetlights
on half-closed eyes in the back seat of a swaying car.
The late night everywhere, oh everywhere
swaying the late occupants in the front seat of the late car.
The late prairies & the late forests,
the cathedral distances between the trees.
The late geography too of the candy counter.
The late six-guns worn calmly to the supper table.
The late fields where we'd play ball,
Ben Nannygoat Carmine Chas Titless Dave & myself,
the late tree under whose branches we'd rest,
the late sun drowning both horizons
in the stock still oceans of the late day,
& the late cry calling Carmine in to eat
whose mother died when her late model Olds
was struck by a pick-up truck crossing the center line
late one night out on the late Corson's Creek Road
before it was widened into Highway 21.
The late high school out there that
is a retirement center now. The late town.
The late wagon wheel ruts beneath the late cobbled streets.
The late forests & the late snow,
& the late sorrow in the late bird's call,

I have heard it falling,
everywhere & forever, the burden of it like a shape beneath the earth
that the moon picks out
to this late elegiac feeling.
The late orchestras playing madly madly on the late radio.
The late bedcovers turned down late in the cold as an apple dark.
The late moon & the late dark,
& the late on & off magic of a late elegy—
there is so much to tell & to tell about it.
I pray I am not too early.

II

WELCOME

Welcome. Ours is a tanager-eyed town.
A tanager-sped, a tanager-topped,
a tanager-held as it were lithesome happenstance,
a wet-browed bird far from the vernacular
of crow's feet fusillades, cocksure as snowdry summaries,
tanager no more,
& if there's something of the cry
of a sleeping tiger tipped sideways in every feather,
something of memory
in the empty branches that says—
what is it, this tanager,
we've never seen one—
Welcome. Welcome home.

BUTTON

Blind old stagehand
to the drama of the human body;
pebble on the shore of the human heart;
but universal cousin; but taciturn nurse;
but unkillable soldier.
Tiny and earless, you lay in laps
in the room full of gossiping women.
Bureaucrat, your head down, double-checking
the rows of numbers.
Strange how there have always been so many of you,
or none; diplomat, able to cross borders
with impunity, familiar to hushed pews,
opulent courts, dim hovels, and smoky camps;
yet in all your family tree, there has never
been a king or poet or general or drunkard or father.
Eunuch, young girls restlessly finger;
face in a crowd; forever banned
from birth and death; worn smooth as a rosary
in the sewing baskets of generations.
O resourceful orphan.
Slave, whose senses have been threaded
by others' desires, until the hard edges of life
break or free you.
It is then you lie among the grasses,
under the stars, or on the sidewalk in the trash and weather,
under the refrigerator, between railroad ties, modern, empty, already a
          mask.

Alone, you invent the desert islands.

Poem Finished on My Birthday

Without the weight
of a heartbeat
that must be given up,
what manner of drop
so prosperous at the edges
now blows through winter's offices
more sleep than rain
old as the new moon—

What you hear
is the stage being set
for things to disappear,
Bob Frost in a grove
his brother Jack has overtaken,
like myself in love
with sagging boughs
that will loose their vows
when summer skies awaken—

Snow on my head
and under my feet
remember me
as one whose nose drips
with the touch of your fingertips,
we'll meet once more
in a downpour of regret
that I am alone
in your throbbing drone
that is the best of us,
even my blood is wet
while it skips—

GIVE ME THE CITY

Give me the city where the streets are poems,
the cars & trucks words constantly
rewriting each line;
bottles & trash along the sidewalks
merely notes, blots, & tentative scrawlings in the margins;
the buildings in each block embodying stanzas

occasionally an ambulance passes through
like an inspiration, while the train
pulling across is writer's block;
a new idea may emerge from a taxi
in the midst of old formal buses;
& the traffic lights are emotions—
giddy rush of ten green in a row
or mounting fury of red after red—who needs them!
a pedestrian must stand bravely
in midstreet like a theme threatened by rhetoric;
the telephone wires are grammatical,
the light poles rhyme;
& manhole covers are words blacked out
maybe to be added later

oh what the rains & snows of time
can do to what we thought was a perfectly good poem!
a tornado render meaningless
the well-intentioned platitudes of a suburb;
floods remind us of speechlessness.
But soon ideas will honk & screech & whine
across the page once more,
little themes squeal & splash along the curb

& the sun come forth to read *SCRIBE*
mainstreet & alley & millionaire moon-curved drive;
in fact in the whole darn book upside down
with what joy illiterate beams write!

Poem for the Inauguration of a President

Now you are president of nothing,
with less power than a city councilman
in a small provincial town. It is not likely
you will give the land
back to the Indians,
or denounce capitalism as it has evolved
for failing to sustain
spiritual values to shape our daily
lives so there is something to model the state on.
I say this because in your campaign
speeches I heard very little of your preparation
for the many years when you would be an
ex-president. And as sure
as evangelists build mansions
or reporters photograph your cat,
you will not place your head on the ground,
in an act of grace, kicking up to balance
with your feet in the air
to show us that you understand
the position you have won.

The Bell

It is not that there is a child inside me,
that is me as I was,
but that there is my part of a child
who is not me, not me
because I can't carry my own coffin.
O happy happy day
when I can no longer hear
people crying over their own coffins.
And part of me sings
O happy happy day.

The Pear Tree

When I was a pear
I bent my branch with song.
I watched the sun sitting on all
his thrones & wore his crown.
I had no thoughts about the lovers
twisted together like roots above the ground,
or the tree that drew itself in the storm & was suddenly gone.
I died with my mouth open

to become a doctor
on his way home at dawn
to his wife who longs for a child.
That was last spring.

Now I pass by the farmer's pear tree,
its branches smooth and bare
as thousands of roads leading from this town.

SETTING THE HARVEST TABLE

somewhere in the tree
Eden's apple asleep
the wide awake ones
come away hunger
come away thirst
neither leaf nor bough the night
nor fruit the day
hang over your orchard's
tended restlessnesses
whatever may fall to happen
there

FISH

I dreamed I didn't have
         to keep swimming:
             I was a fish.
   Ah it was lonely, lonely
         caught by the moon's hair
             & the ocean's laughter
         soft as sand waking a sailor:
              touching that's all—

         Somewhere in a boat
         with such a desire
            to fool water

POEM

I don't get old men trying to be older,
reaching into pasts farther than their stories,
refashioning,
scrubbing their shadows with cheer like bodies with sand,   *BLEACH*
unnatural,
I thought it was childhood
returns with the accumulation of years,
we'd burn through history
before the afternoon had got its tan,
fought all the wars
(& invented new ones),
slept in caves & nursed fire,
looked back at the future
(saw the birth of stars),
& came home on feet
able to track mud
from their fossilized prints
across our mothers' carpets,
it was serious
        as long as it was fun,
important
        as long as it was easy,
come join us if not in fields & forests
then roadside ditches
where medals come in harvests,
enough to throw your shirt away
daily & not go without plumage.
I'm told your chests are puffed out
FROM for harboring so much death
that it is difficult to breathe,
STILL now youth would know why for old men
being old is a labor.

Fall

Rabbit & moon & bonfire
        lashing sparks into the air
  Gone, leaving a patch
       of night starless on the ground
  Gone, to whet the milk-tooth
       of a hound
  Gone, like a liar in the sun
       drowned in the well of the ear
    such a little fire, sister,
    such a little fire
  Gone, but it is still there

Brief Aubade

to the
architect
of night:
does your
antiquity
never tire—
I would sleep—
from what babel
you tower
does not matter
though even one floor
might mean
there are
lights to come—
like silence
that invents the drum—

but I must nod
& dream
my labors
have ended
after a
dizzying climb—
I would sleep
and wake cold—
there is no door
opened
by starshorn laughter
the architecture of
delirium
has yet to utter—
morning
your goodbye—
more than
window
can hold

STREETSINGER

That coat the cricket wore fits me now,
so many buttons of a laugh against the cold.
Hats in the pepper, my breath in the sea,
I stand up in this fashion,
no more far-fetched than fire,
the ends of my scarf
wrapped around the body of Socrates,
and blind, blind, blind, blind….

Before summer dies, if it ever
comes again, I would loose
fugitive skies & live
like shoelaces—an elemental man
wearing someone else's coat—what are years
but the bottoms of the bridges in the river's eyes.

The Old Lamplighter

Monday. Another workday
compacted like two
and a half decades

into a cake
the size of a giant old tin gargoyle encrusted
matchbox, heavy enough

to pass into the bowels
of the earth. Candles soon—
bridge lifted

over the moat,
a meal simple enough too—
platter of angels' thighs,

and fairy wings
forked from a bowl,
quaffs from a bottle

Stephen Crane knew,
its label the face
you make when you swallow.

Soon, soon enough
candles & bed.
Off with the feet

and head. The
old lamplighter is home.
How many horses

in your town?
Their nostrils full
of smoke, their manes
horribly tossing light,

O how many galloping
three legged horses
in your far towns?

QUICKLY AGING HERE

You wake up
   color tv blaring
      to find you're Emily Dickinson.

  Sure, you feel the cathedral spaces
    between the trees,
        the cold,
  and know how to look a dragonfly
     in the eye
     But you're two-hundred years old—

   And the world is worried
     as wrinkled-up panties
         in the street—
    The touch of your hand
      can turn a baby's hair white as sleet—

 Come storm, deliver
   your rains, I hear Celtic, Urdu, Greek
    against the panes, I've a never fear, a fever shiver—
     I'm aging fast Emily—
     Am I drunk now, really drunk at last—
    or hopelessly sunk
      in Li Po's river?

III

Atget Photographs the Palace at Versailles, 1901

Marble clouds of stairs, chiseled balconies in an April sky,
the king inside, his heart hollow as the hallways
so high & deep bread baked nearly long as ladders
can't reach him, no royal rain to fall
on his loyal lands, no sighs from Versailles,
just polished stone that floats over the trees & Eugene,
invisible there as always as the sun's rays
rooted in the earth scraped by so many knees,
his countrymen can only know an ugly awkward apparatus
on three legs & a patient simpleton perhaps,
not miles of massive opulence, ornate iron & glass
insubstantial as a speck of dust containing many rooms,
in one of them a king, vivre le France, Eugene,
in so many hearts a song.

FRANKENSTEIN II

Dear father,

     I drink my soup without
        spilling very much and am good
           though I have not yet found a place
             between the birds & fishes.

    Sometimes I tire of clearing
       the roads of fallen timber
          and cutting & stacking it near
            one or another farmhouse.

    But how else to repay
       the tools & meager stores
         of food & clothing that
             I would otherwise be stealing.

    Even when I stay hidden
       as you have advised,
          I know that I am not alone.
          I have seen my self

more often than anyone supposes,
       shrinking from the moonlight,
           though I have also known tiny fluttering
              things come as to a petal in sunlight

your hand, father. I know
       I am not the only one
          to hear cries in the night
            that make my heart feel

my heart. This is not my first April.
    And I hope at least one villager,
       like the flowers, holds on to his torch
          until he has burned his fingers.

Jazz Lullaby

trumpets are locomotives, caskets with polished windows,
a gat made completely from compass needles,
trombones are descendants of sober aerialists
in drunken circuses, tenor saxophones are radiators,
while alto saxophones have hummingbird wings added,
clarinets are hatracks in foreign lands,
pianos are expensive hotels in the poor
part of town, drums are weddings and funerals,
divorces and exhumations, railroad trains without tracks,
basses are smoke over cool water, light suddenly shone
on midnight, unclimbed mountains, guitars are souvenir shops
gypsies can empty so fast

in what place are they together
without surreality, but song—

sleep must follow attentively, so much sleep—
abandoned by the would-be sleepers—

so many roads are wrong
that have overtaken song

SPRING

dear frog,
ever since you jumped in the pond,
and that man heard,
he has reached through the fog
of years as with a wand
made of dragonflywing,
to tell me that spring
is inside me & can always be stirred

forget it, forget it, forget it, forget it
all that rhyme, Tom,
locks your summer in ice,
poetry squats green & big-eyed
in swirls of cloud & silence,
in sloppy froth the cows will crop,
you cold & naked,
without a word to find you,
on this disturbing farm,
waiting for basho

Dirty Song

It's always the same,
    I just want to see,
Mommy and daddy,
    you making me.

Am I wind, the snow,
    (I want to be),
Grandma and grandpa,
    footsteps leading to the sea…

The waves clap hands,
    they keep weird time,
The clocks trouble
    their jewels endlessly…

WORLD, YOU ARE LIKE

nor any canyons
natural or built
world, you are like
a few miles out
from a Midwest town
flat as the aisle
in a five-and-dime
your dark is lit
—neither day or night
having not
said a word—
the shadow
of voiceless noon
laid out on the snow
in your wake
some, not me,
would call you back,
world,
I'm tired of your echoes
about to speak

TREES

Tent the sky, umbrella the rain,
ignore those many feet, pilgrim sought & bound—
you rooted in air, wet with stars,
breathless pause where the dance is gathered—
(what kind of thinking is it
with every thought present—)
I have sat arrogant as apples beside you
untouched by your fingerprint of leaves—
but you have hands enough
        to play sleep's castanets
           & build the night

build the night, trophy the sun,
island the shipwrecked snows—
while it's enthralling dark to which I am led,
that hides birth & death under outstretched joys & sorrows,
      I find like love, like wind, after a long day in the wood
        you might wake up beneath a tree
           different from the one
              where you lay your head

CHINESE JUNK

Origami mirror for what
swims beneath the waters
it glides upon—

More rope than smoke,
more fin than sail,
& more timber

than is in the houses
those on board
ran away from—

Hatches everywhere—
On ashtrays never to be used,
hand-painted oceans

submerged in excelsior
lashed into darkness
guarded by drugged rats—

Golden soups,
hair woven into fish,
ribs folded on

moonless decks,
untranslatable ladders,
the captain asleep

while tarpaulins fill
with alarm clocks
set for the first day

of barber college—
Strange harbors
in the crewmen's eyes....

Kafka Country

winter has driven the surface from the lake
has driven jumping from the frogs
has driven narcissus from himself
now is what patience looks like
to the impatient
gestures of a dying limb
& color dying in the face of things
the wind stabbing
each lonely piece of coal
hunger teaching ribs its calligraphy
& scat frozen to the ground
the sun's honey stopped in its throat
unable to pour
in the cold dark of its constitution
only the law growing fatter
behind its grate of marble columns
one more book bulging & rebound
with the story
of the wolf who ate fire

WOLVES   THE

Props

Rain to balance
cold & warm,
rain is homeless
in a storm,

flood with a mind
for murder,
woman before
there is a daughter,

spills the moonlight
into sand,
sifts the stars
within the hand,

turns the snow
into flowers,
hides away
all the hours,

finishes what I start.
Storm, storm, heart
to the bone,
you were born wet

    & will die,
thunder like
    tin sheeting,
rain like rice thrown.

WINTER

And if that's not summer enough....
a gathering of shadows....
Distant. Tribal. Home. Winter.
Where else but somewhere.... *SOME WHERE....*
Going farther away....

THE ALBINO JUGGLER

while falling
ask the snow
where it is
child
& before I could
anything
the Albino Juggler
said up
is what I thought
I heard
now it
is
gone
sun and sky
tossed
above the ground
below my feet
not likely
to come down
or show me
in whose hands
he goes on
floating
the worlds
some June or July
I'll soon
enough
come to
meet *FOLLOW*

48

Heart Carved from Wood

In the tree it didn't seem human,
or when marshaled into armies of uniform size
to house hearts of men,
the rain-beat found it,
wind brought back memory of the saw,
and the grain inside & out
carried us like a river into knotless lands…

…but horrible to see the imagined contours
& hold it reft—
like adding handles to the knives in the blood—
an Aztec air then & now—
scars the nostrils uncover—
a secret vein opens
& out pour hands!

There are Trains, Willie

There are trains, Willie,
longer than a step away from the earth
the winds & grackle winds come back from, Mary,
the snow-bound rails the summer cars
full of grass's shadow now lightning now drums, Willie,
brakemen buried in the blood raise their lanterns
to an only cry for
where they pass, Mary,
a wild throw of ticket-stubs around the stations
of dust at your feet & still the lights come on, Willie,
& no one gets off,
the platforms crumbling & excited, *EXCITING*
the trains longer than a step away from the earth.

POEM

for Cathy Anderson

The snow's cry ends with the owl's cry
like something green
after all that has fallen

like flowers that hide
from the gardener forever
his favorite trowel and shovel

like a full-moon earth
that leaves behind
all the hours

for clown's make-up
senseless as green buttons in green owls
until laughter's cry ends

O it does end,
it does end
like the storm's cry that ends

with summer's cry
wild and yellow
in monstrous apples

as the body's cry ends with the child's cry
at the snow's sparkling like something green
so many have fallen

About the Author

Thomas Zemsky was born in Hamilton, Ohio in 1947. He received his MFA from the Iowa Writers' Workshop. Since 1976 he has made his home in Lexington, Kentucky where he worked for many years for the International Book Project. Now retired, his favorite pastimes include listening to jazz on LP records, Latin American and modern literature, and movies according to the auteur theory. He believes that poetry, first and foremost, is metaphor. This is his first book.